RACING TO INDY

Author

Mike Kupper

Photography

Heinz Kluetmeier
Bob D'Olivo

Published by   **Advanced Learning Concepts, Inc.**
Milwaukee, Wisconsin

A Product of   **Advanced Learning Concepts, Inc.**
and Follett Publishing Company
A Division of Follett Corporation
Chicago, Illinois

Contents

1
The Drivers

Around and around they went. Three cars, so close together they might have been one. Racing for lap after lap. Racing at well over one hundred miles an hour on the mile track at Milwaukee's State Fair Park.

Rodger Ward, a two-time winner at Indianapolis, was in the lead. Right behind him was A. J. Foyt. Foyt had already won twice at Indianapolis. He would win again before he was through, and was well on his way to becoming the finest all-around American race driver ever. Running third was Jim Hurtubise, a driver of great promise. Many considered him Foyt's main rival in the years to come.

Three men, each very different from the others. Ward, smooth and polished, easy to like. Foyt, rough-cut and direct, yet distant and hard to know. Hurtubise, happy-go-lucky and friendly, but quick tempered and changeable.

Three men, each very different from the others. But three men determined to do the same thing, win the same prize.

Obviously only one could win. Something had to happen. In racing, something usually does. It may be something as simple as a flat tire. A driver may run his car out of fuel. One

The Indy 500 — Start To Finish

Preparing the cars, the time trials, the drivers and fans, start of the race, in the pits, a fiery wreck, the winner's trophy

may be quicker than the others during a pit stop, thanks to a good, fast crew. Or one may simply use superior skill or a slightly faster car to outrun the others.

As the three cars came out of the fourth turn and headed down the main straightaway, still tightly bunched, Ward's lead car developed transmission trouble. Knowing that his speed would drop quickly, he raised his left hand to warn Foyt and Hurtubise that he was slowing.

Foyt hit the brakes and swerved away from Ward's powerless car. Hurtubise was not so lucky. His car bumped the rear of Foyt's car, then took off and sailed over the top of it, just missing Foyt's head.

"I just looked up and there he was, going over the top of me," Foyt said.

Hurtubise's car sailed into the concrete wall at the outside edge of the track. It burst into flames and rolled to the top of the straightaway. The jolt when the car hit the wall had left Hurtubise unconscious. He could not get out of the burning car by himself. By the time the rescue crew got to him, he had suffered severe burns over nearly half his body. Burns on his face and hands were especially bad.

He would live, but he would be terribly scarred. He would race again, too. But he would never reach the heights predicted for him.

Ward? He would continue racing for two more years, then retire suddenly during the Indianapolis 500, saying later that racing was no longer fun for him.

And Foyt? Foyt went on to win the race that day. And he went on to win a lot more than that. His friend, Hurtubise, had been seriously injured. Foyt felt terrible about that. But Foyt had won the race, and he felt good about that.

His statements afterward were signals of his mixed emotions.

"We were going into that turn too fast and too tight for this kind of track," he said. "If all the races are going to be this hairy, I may consider quitting."

Less than an hour later, though, he was remembering the race before the accident. "That was some racing. Wasn't that some racing? You ever see racing like that?"

Later, when everything was over at the track, Foyt joined other drivers at the hospital, waiting for word on Hurtubise. Some still were dressed in their driving suits. Their faces still were caked with track grime. Foyt had showered and changed clothes. He looked fresh.

It was Foyt who thought to ask if Hurtubise needed money. And Foyt who thought to ask if Hurtubise's wife had been told of the accident, to ask if anything could be done for her.

Race drivers often are portrayed as superhuman figures, with just the barest resemblance to everybody else. If anything, though, race drivers are extremely human.

Scientific studies have been made on them. The results are almost always the same. They show race drivers to have especially good eyesight, and especially good reflexes. They show that race drivers tend to be less dependent, less friendly than most people. They show that race drivers are proud athletes who have an intense desire to win. And they show that race drivers tend to be small.

What those studies have done is given us a "typical" driver. And there really is no such thing. Drivers are highly individualized.

Some, such as Joe Leonard and Mike Mosley, wear eyeglasses. Some, such as Lloyd Ruby and Mel Kenyon, are easygoing and friendly. Most want to win, but some are

satisfied just to compete. They are proud, but most go to great pains to share with the crew the credit for a victory.

Although many of them are small, compared to athletes in other sports, there are exceptions. Dan Gurney stands well over six feet. And Foyt, with his stocky frame, would make a pretty good middleweight boxer.

Mario Andretti, who is small, figures he's pretty typical.

"How come everyone always refers to me as jockey-sized?" he asked once.

"How come nobody ever describes me as race-driver-sized?"

2
The Cruel Sport

Of all sports, automobile racing probably is the least understood. It is not played with a ball or a stick or a racquet, the way most popular games are.

It is done with cars, cars that are powerful, fast, and often temperamental.There are cars built especially for racing. They are the thoroughbreds of the auto racing world. And there are cars racing that were never meant to be raced. They are much different from the thoroughbreds, but they are raced just the same.

There is no typical playing field. A racetrack may be as short as one-fifth of a mile. Or it may be as long as fifteen miles. It may be paved, usually with asphalt. Or it may be dirt, usually a gummy clay. It may have a well-defined shape, such as an oval, a rounded square, or the shape of a huge letter D. Or it may resemble a country road. It may be nearly flat, with only left-hand turns. It may be steeply banked, with only left-hand turns. It may go up and down hills, with turns both left and right.

There is no typical race car, either. There are championship cars, the kind that race each year in the Indianapolis 500. There are sprint cars. There are midget cars. There are at least four types of stock cars. There are

sports cars and formula cars. And there is a whole different world of drag racing cars.

The variety may be exciting to some. To many others, it is only confusing.

The many groups that regulate racing can also be confusing. There is at least one group for every kind of racing done in the United States, Canada, Europe, South America, Australia, and parts of Asia. And each group usually has its own rules.

It's no secret that auto racing can be very dangerous. In most sports, the penalty for a mistake is often defeat. Sometimes, a mistake can result in serious injury. In auto racing, a mistake often results in death, sometimes several deaths at a time. Dan Gurney, who used to race before he began building cars, once called racing "the cruel sport." Death in racing is accepted as a distasteful part of the game. And it shows no respect for age, rank, talent, or the type of accident.

Young and promising drivers, such as Bobby Marshman and Dave MacDonald, have been killed in racing crashes, almost before their careers had begun. Successful veteran drivers, such as Bill Vukovich, Tony Bettenhausen, and Don Branson, have been killed in racing crashes, long after they have proven their competence. The threat of death in racing is ever present and no one is immune.

Often there is a lull. A season, two seasons maybe, will go by and nobody will be killed. Then death will strike like a thunderclap, taking one, two, maybe three or more in a single race.

In 1973, Art Pollard died after crashing into a wall the morning of qualifying for the Indianapolis 500. In the race that followed, driver Swede Savage was critically injured in an accident, and a pit worker was killed when he was run down by an emergency vehicle hurrying to the site of Savage's crash. Savage later died of his injuries.

A cruel sport, indeed.

And yet, auto racing thrives. Something about it appeals to people. Auto racing, in all of its forms, attracts more spectators year after year than any other sport but horse racing.

So what is it that makes auto racing attractive? Is it speed? That certainly must be a part of it. Is it the cars themselves? That, too, surely must be a part of it. Is it the danger? Partly.

The real answer goes much deeper than any of those, though. In fact, it goes back almost to the beginning of mankind.

Stone Age people were hunters. Sometimes, to make sure of a meal, they had to run their prey to exhaustion. Sometimes, too, they had to run for their lives. Somewhere in the depths of history, someone probably wondered about running faster than the others in the tribe. They raced.

People have been racing ever since. At first it was just foot racing. Then the horse was tamed, and people raced on horseback. Probably about two days after the invention of the wheel, somebody had figured out some way to attach it to something for racing. And auto racing is just an extension of the desire for competition.

For that's what is at the root of auto racing. It's speed and snorting, roaring cars and danger. It's all of these things and more.

It is the driver and machine working together until they are one.

Put together several of the car-driver combinations, and you have the makings of a race. And suddenly, racing isn't confusing anymore. It is — pure and simple — competition.

That's why as many as three hundred thousand people pack the Indianapolis Motor Speedway for the one race that is

held there each year. That's why some people who have no real interest in sports or athletics will listen to the radio the afternoon of the Indianapolis race. They may not care about racing, but they want to know who won.

For many of those who are not racing fans, the racing season begins and ends with that one race, the Indianapolis 500. For anybody who is in racing, or connected with it, however, there is more. Much more. The Indianapolis 500 may be the big race of the year in the United States, but it is only the biggest of many. These races make up what is formally known as championship car racing. To most people, though, it carries the nickname of the big race itself. It is simply called Indy racing.

3
The Indy Car Circuit

The Arizona desert is cool in the early morning March air. Overhead, a vulture glides on silent wings. All is silence.

Then, off in the distance, an engine crackles to life. Another throaty voice joins in. Soon the stillness of the desert is no more. Now the desert air throbs, pulses, screams, and roars as it carries the sounds of thirty or more race cars.

Desert? Race cars?

Indeed! For Indy car racing is done where the tracks are, whether in desert or big city.

There is a track at Ontario, California, on the West Coast, and one at Trenton, New Jersey, on the Eastern Seaboard. In between are the tracks at Phoenix, Arizona; Milwaukee, Wisconsin; Indianapolis, Indiana; Cambridge Junction, Michigan; and Mount Pocono, Pennsylvania. It is those tracks that make up the Indy car circuit. Sometimes other tracks are added for a while. One year an Indy car race was seen in Argentina. Another year, racing fans in Japan got a chance to see what Indy racing was all about.

The Indy car circuit, or championship trail, winds its way across the country and back again during the course of a season. The season, which runs roughly from early

23

March to early November, is under the direction of the United States Auto Club.

USAC, as the United States Auto Club is popularly called, is one of several main race-sanctioning bodies in the United States. It is, in some ways, like the American League in baseball, the National Football League, or the National Basketball Association.

USAC decides which tracks will have its races and which drivers are capable of driving in them. USAC runs races in five divisions. It has a division for late model stock cars and a division for sprint cars. It has a division for midget cars and a division for older-style Indy cars that race strictly on dirt tracks.

First and foremost, however, it has the Indy cars. And no other race-sanctioning group in the world can make that statement. You can race stocks, sprinters, midgets, or dirt trackers in any number of other organizations. If you want to race Indy cars, though, you can only do it in USAC.

Phoenix, Trenton, Milwaukee, and the Michigan International Speedway at Cambridge Junction usually get two races a season. They are the smaller tracks in USAC; and their races are shorter than on the long tracks at Ontario, Indianapolis, and Mount Pocono. Indy car races are run once a year at the three big tracks, and all are five-hundred-mile events.

There is no easing into the new season. It starts with a five-hundred-mile race at the Ontario Motor Speedway in early March. The Ontario track is almost a direct copy of the Indianapolis Speedway. It is two-and-a-half miles around and shaped like a rectangle with rounded corners. The track surface itself is much wider than the track at Indianapolis, and about sixty years newer.

To spectators, the Ontario track may look like Indianapolis West. But drivers point out that the resemblance is only in the eye.

Those who have driven both say that they are no more similar than apples and oranges. Each, they say, has its own character. And each must be driven differently.

From Ontario, the circuit moves to the Phoenix FasTrack. The track was built several miles out of town in the Arizona desert. It is not unusual to see a cowboy astride his horse on the top of a nearby hill, casually watching the racetrack drama below.

The Phoenix track is the only one of its kind on the Indy car circuit. It is a mile around, shaped like a D. Its unusual shape gives it two very sharp turns, a long sweeping bend around the back, and just one straightaway. It is not as fast as the longer tracks, but drivers say it is very demanding.

By mid-April, the circuit has moved east to Trenton's one-and-one-half-mile track at the New Jersey State Fairgrounds. Trenton, in its early days, was a twin to the track at Milwaukee. It was a nearly flat, one-mile oval with two straights and two turns.

Now it has a character all its own, and something seen nowhere else on the circuit. When the track was made longer, a kink was put into the backstretch. It served two purposes. It made it possible to make the track longer in a limited area. And, because this was done only on the backstretch, it keeps drivers from reaching speeds too high for safe driving through the turn to the main straight.

In European road racing, such kinks are common. But Trenton has the only one on the Indy circuit. And that means it is the only track on the circuit where drivers must make a right-hand turn.

Once the Trenton race is over, the focus shifts to Indianapolis, where all of May is spent preparing for the 500 at the end of the month, during the Memorial Day weekend. It may seem that the preparation time for one race is overdone, but everyone has a simple

Reading LAB

explanantion for that. "It's Indianapolis," they say with a shrug.

And indeed it is. The most glamorous race at the best known track, with the biggest payoff of any race in the world. So much prestige and instant wealth are attached to the winning of the 500 that even European road racers frequently are eager to compete. And that is quite a concession for them, since normally they have little to do with what has come to be known as American oval-track racing.

The track at Indianapolis was not built for racing at all, but rather as a test area for early car manufacturers who had their plants in or near Indianapolis. In 1911, it was decided that a good way to test cars would be to race them for five hundred miles. The Indianapolis 500 was born; and Ray Harroun, driving a Marmon Wasp, won the first five-hundred-mile race over the two-and-a-half-mile, brick-paved track.

The idea caught on and grew, and now the Indianapolis 500 is the greatest-drawing single event in the sports world. The old bricks are gone, and tons of asphalt have replaced them. But the track is still the same two-and-a-half-mile, rounded rectangle that it was in 1911. And if the people in racing have anything to say about it, it always will be. It's Indianapolis.

From Indianapolis, it's on to Milwaukee's one-mile track, a track that looks easy. It isn't. It is a straightforward track with no tricks — just two straights connected by two nearly flat corners. Drivers who take it for granted soon learn that it has its own nature and must be driven with care.

Gordon Johncock got a strong reminder of that one Sunday afternoon in August of 1973. Johncock was well on his way to victory in the annual Tony Bettenhausen Memorial 200 there, having driven his car to an eleven-second lead.

29

Going into the north turn, however, he cut the corner short, trying to get another lap on the slower moving car of Johnny Rutherford by passing on the inside. Johncock lost the precise control he needed for just a fraction of a second, but that was all that was required to mess up his day. Instead of rolling smoothly through the turn, his car slid out and he hit Rutherford from behind. Neither driver was hurt, but Johncock's car was badly damaged. There was no big payoff for him that day.

The rolling country of the Pocono Mountains in Pennsylvania is next, for another five-hundred-miler at the Pocono International Speedway. It, too, is an unusual track, for it is a triangle. More than that, it is an unbalanced triangle. None of the three straights is the same length as the others. None of the three corners matches the others. It is a tough test for driver and machine.

Next, there is the Michigan International Speedway at Cambridge Junction in an area of Michigan known as Irish Hills. It is two miles long, but the corners are banked. This gives the drivers an extra boost of speed where they are used to slowing down.

After Michigan, it's back to Milwaukee for a race in August and back to Trenton and Michigan again for races in September. Then finally back to Phoenix for a race in late October or early November.

Each race on the circuit is a separate event, with its own payoff. But each has another meaning, too. Points are earned, on a sliding scale according to distance, by the first twelve drivers in each race. The winner gets two points per mile, the second place driver 1.8 points per mile, and so on down the line.

At the end of the season, the driver with the most points is recognized as the national driving champion of the United States.

4
Who's Got the Money?

Indy car racing is a big money sport, any way you look at it. There is plenty of money to be made.

But there is a hitch. Usually it takes plenty of money to get into a position to go after the bigger money.

The big exception to that general rule is the driver. With plenty of talent, plenty of nerve, intelligence, and the opportunity to show these qualities, the driver can become a millionaire in just a few years. One of the biggest problems is staying alive long enough to make talent and nerve pay off.

Still, there are a lot of drivers around who are not only alive, but wealthy as well. A lot of that wealth comes from deals they have made in the fringe areas of racing. But in most cases, the start of the bankroll came directly from racing.

Most obvious to the casual fan is the money the drivers are racing for in any particular event. In racing, it's called a purse. In USAC's Indy car racing, the purse is divided by all who qualify for starting positions in the race itself. The winner may get as much as one-third of the total purse, and the last place driver as little as a few hundred dollars. But everyone in the race gets something.

Everybody loves a winner, though, and the big money is up front, at the head of the field. That is one of the obvious reasons that drivers try hard to win. In some races there is also lap money, a special prize paid to the leader of each lap.

Even so, in every race there will be a fair-sized number of cars and drivers who could win only on the flukiest chance. Instead of trying to win, their object is to finish the race. That way, they can almost be assured of a finishing spot in the first half of the field, where the money is better.

A driver who almost always drives to win is known as a charger. One who almost always drives just to finish is known as a stroker. And one who is a notorious stroker is known as a C & C driver — C & C for "coast and collect."

Even the purse money is misleading, though. Say an event has a $100,000 purse, and first place money is $25,000. That first place money does not go directly to the driver, but to the racing team. The driver gets a share, usually half or less, from the team manager or car owner.

A driver who is new on the circuit may have all the talent in the world, but will still have to win a number of times before getting into the big money. A driver's contract probably will call for nothing more than a split of whatever prize money the whole team collects.

Once a driver has become known as a smart, fast driver who usually finishes in the top six or seven, though, there are plenty of people who are eager to offer a better contract or just more money.

A contract with a team, for instance, may call for a yearly salary, a fifty percent split of prize money, and bonuses for winning a 500 or the national championship. Sometimes drivers make enough that way to buy their own equipment and set up their own teams.

Then, if they win, they collect all the prize money.

And for the successful driver, there are always other sources of income. There is money from sponsors and money from personal appearances. There is money from companies wanting an endorsement for their products. There is money from other companies for using their equipment exclusively. And there is money from places where young drivers didn't know there was money.

For almost everyone else in racing, though, money is a constant source of concern.

Indy cars are expensive to build or buy, and even more expensive to keep in top racing trim. An they don't last long. The wonder car of last year is very likely to be obsolete now.

"I'm the only car owner who ever made any money racing," Andy Granatelli once boasted, though he may have been stretching a little. J. C. Agajanian, a long-time car owner whose drivers won the Indianapolis 500 twice, finally quit because of the high cost of equipment and mechanical help. Lindsey Hopkins, another veteran car owner, long ago gave up the idea of making money on his cars. "I do it for fun," he says. "Racing is my sport, and I support it by owning cars. It's my hobby, something I enjoy doing. If I make money, that's fine, but mostly I do it for fun." Hopkins, a millionaire several times over, can afford that kind of fun.

Many others can't, and there is a constant scramble for sponsors who will foot the bill or share it with a racing team. Some sponsorships, a very few, are total. Most, though, are partial. And that accounts for the seemingly endless number of decals pasted onto nearly every USAC championship car. Companies pay teams to use, and advertise, their products.

And then there are the tire companies. Without at least one tire company up to its hubcaps in racing, it is doubtful that USAC Indy

car racing could survive.

In racing, the tire companies are the great subsidizers. For more than fifty years, Firestone was so closely associated with racing that its most famous lines of tires were known as the Firestone Champion and Firestone 500.

The company had a separate racing tire division that operated under the belief that having the Firestone name in front of the public was good, and that if a tire was good on the racetrack, it would be even better on the highway.

Firestone rented tracks and paid accomplished race drivers to test their racing tires. It gave tires away or sold them at huge discounts. And it bailed out teams in financial trouble.

Then Goodyear, a much larger company, got into the act. For a number of years, there was spirited competition between the companies. Money was practically showered upon drivers and racing teams for their loyalty to one company or the other. Nylon windbreakers were the uniform of the day at every track. Blue with gold script for Goodyear, red with white lettering for Firestone.

In at least one case, it led to an amusing situation. Brothers Bobby and Al Unser, driving for different teams, used different brands of tires. One day their father showed up at the Indianapolis Speedway with a windbreaker, half blue and half red. And on the back, it read FIREYEAR. Mom Unser, the mother of Bobby and Al, had one just like it, except that on the back it said GOODSTONE.

In little more than ten years, though, Goodyear had forced Firestone to reconsider. When the reconsideration was made, Firestone was out of racing and Goodyear had the field to itself. That may have been a plus for Goodyear, but it was a minus for

racing, since it meant that less money was available.

It also meant, in some cases, that some racing teams ceased to exist, since many cars had been secretly owned by one company or the other.

Even under the best circumstances, owning a race car, or a stable of race cars, is a risky business. The poor teams haven't the money to buy top equipment or hire top mechanics and drivers. And the successful teams usually are forced to plow their money back into development to stay ahead of, or even with, the competition.

The cost of fielding a team at Indianapolis alone is astronomical. A single car, one of the good ones or one of the new ones on which development costs have been lavished, may easily be worth more than $100,000. The average figure is less than that, somewhere from $75,000 to $80,000, and some of the older cars may be worth no more than $40,000. But with the cost of engines alone running at about $25,000 apiece, none of them is cheap.

And the cost of a single car is only the surface figure. Each must have spare engines, along with assorted spare parts. The top teams usually have a backup car for each car entered, so the cost is doubled. There are the salaries of the driver and crew to be paid. And there is the motel bill of the crew for a month. It's not cheap, even for the lesser teams. The owner of the winning Indianapolis car will break even, if he's lucky.

5
My Team, Your Team

When most people go to an Indy car race, the things they notice are cars and drivers.

The brightly colored cars are shiny. Even while standing still they have about them the feeling of speed.

The drivers are cool and detached in their fire-retardant white suits. Confident as they walk the pit area, they are thought of by many as modern-day gladiators.

But it takes more than cars and drivers to make a race.

Knowledgable fans know that chief mechanics, car designers, team managers, and pit crews usually have as much to do with success or failure as the drivers.

It wasn't always that way. In the early days of racing, it was a much simpler business. Someone bought a car, usually just an ordinary manufacturer's car, modified it slightly for racing, and hired a driver. Or, the owner drove the car. In those days, it was simply auto racing, and the cars that were being raced were very much like the cars that sent the chickens flying on the back country roads.

Even in the beginning, though, the racetrack was a meeting place for people with mechan-

43

ical genius. They could see, in the cars of their day, the hundreds of areas that needed improvement. So they improved their cars.

And people have been improving and making changes in cars ever since, until they have developed a single-purpose thoroughbred. You can't, for example, carry the groceries home from the supermarket in an Indy car, for the simple reason that you can't drive the car there. At city street speeds, the spark plugs would foul in the car's own oil within a few blocks.

Indy cars have just one reason for existence — racing.

And they no longer are built and maintained by mechanics tinkering around in the backyard. They need the best care that can be given by a small army of people with tedious, difficult jobs.

Just as there really is no such thing as a typical driver, there also is no such thing as a typical racing team. Each has several things in common with the others, but each has a different makeup and does certain things in different ways.

The first thing a racing team needs is someone to supervise the organization — a car owner or team manager. Sometimes the car owner is also the car designer, chief mechanic, and, in rare instances, the driver. That team, though, is likely to be short of cash and probably will have rough going.

Sometimes, too, the car owner will put up the money, then hire a team manager, or a chief mechanic who doubles as team manager, and put this person in charge of the operation.

The next decision concerns the main piece of equipment, the car. "Shall we build our own, or buy one and rebuild it to our liking?"

That decision depends on just how much money is available to a team. Some buy,

some build, some rebuild, some do a little of everything. There is one thing that has become one of the truths of racing. In any year, at any track, most of the cars are going to look just about like the rest of the cars. In racing, copycatting is one of the big sidelines. Everybody is looking for the "hot setup"; and when one team finds it, the others will latch onto it.

For a team planning to buy a new car, there are several options. There are European factories that specialize in race car design and building. A car owner may go to any one of them and strike up a deal.

Or an owner may choose to buy from one of the American racing teams that designs and builds its own cars. Thus Dan Gurney not only fields a team of cars for himself and his sponsor, but also builds cars to sell to other teams. The less wealthy teams usually have to make do with last year's car, or somebody else's last year's car.

Other teams, those rich enough to afford it, hire designers, build their own cars and race them, not selling to anyone else. They may sell their cars next season, but by then they will have found ways to improve. Usually, they keep the improvements to themselves, selling last year's version of the car to customers.

As with most things in racing, car design is a risky proposition. In the late 1950s and early 1960s, A. J. Watson was the ranking car designer and mechanic. He not only built for his team, but sold to to others besides. The watchword then was, "If you haven't got a Watson, you haven't got a chance."

In those days, the Indy cars were of the roadster design. They were low-slung, heavy cars with front-mounted engines. Then suddenly, they were obsolete.

Winds of change came blowing across the Atlantic Ocean from Europe. Road racing teams there had discovered that light cars

with engines in the rear were much better than heavy cars with the engines in front.

Colin Chapman of the Lotus racing organization in England entered two of his light, rear-engine cars in the 1963 Indianapolis 500, against the heavy cars that had dominated Indianapolis for so many years. Driving for Chapman were Dan Gurney and Jim Clark. Most of the American teams gave the British team little chance. "Too fragile," they said of the spidery new cars. "They won't last."

But they did last. Clark finished second to Parnelli Jones' big roadster, and Gurney was seventh. The handwriting was on the wall when Clark won and Gurney finished third in a two-hundred-mile race at Milwaukee later that season in the new-style car. The stampede was on. Within two seasons the lightweight rear-engine car had replaced the heavy front-engine roadster.

As for Watson, he tried to make the changeover, too. But his rear-engine cars never were as good as his front-engine roadsters. He finally gave up building his own. He stayed in racing, and his genius with engines was still recognized; but nobody came to him for cars anymore.

Although race cars are made up of thousands of parts, they come in two basic components — the chassis (that is, the body and suspension system) and the engine. On the struggling teams, the chief mechanic may have to attend to problems in both areas. The wealthier teams will have a mechanic, who works only on the engine, and a chassis expert, whose job is to cure the car's ills in that area. There also will be assistants doing a little bit of everything.

If a team is maintaining several cars for several drivers, the chief mechanic will have a greater number of assistants. Sometimes each car will have its own crew. Sometimes, too, the entire crew will work on all of the

cars in that particular stable. On race day, the mechanical staff stays in the pits, servicing the car as needed during pit stops. Quick stops are preferred. The less time a car spends in the pits, the more time it can be running on the track at racing speed, which in Indy car races approaches two hundred miles an hour.

Because there is so little time for major repairs during a race, a car that develops a serious problem is either pulled out or allowed to finish as best it can. Pit work normally amounts to refueling and changing tires. A good crew can do those chores in less than half a minute.

Sometimes an overeager crew can do more harm than good. A partially filled fuel tank, or a wheel that is only partially tightened will cause an unscheduled pit stop, maybe an accident.

An overeager crew probably cost Lloyd Ruby a victory in the 1969 Indianapolis 500.

Ruby, a notoriously poor qualifier, started the race far down the lineup, in the twentieth position. Driving bravely and skillfully, he weaved his way through the pack. By the halfway point, he was running only two seconds behind the leader, Mario Andretti. When Andretti stopped for fuel a few laps later, Ruby inherited the lead.

His fuel was running low, however, and he had to stop. He pulled into his pit and, after a short delay, got a tap on the back of his helmet, the signal that it was time for him to be on his way.

Ruby began to pull away, but in its haste the crew had neglected to disconnect one of the refueling nozzles from the car. The coupling remained firm, pulling the mouth of the fuel tank off the car. Fuel gushed out of the hole in the side of the tank and Ruby stopped, peering over the side to see what had happened.

59
69
4
2 20
2 8
5 84
6 98
44
13
60
3
19
48
6
24
66
5
35
16
2
1
89
62
30
9
40
16
12
18
14
28
12
11

51

Shaking his head, he slumped down into the cockpit, then finally clambered out of the car. He removed his helmet and, without a word to the crew, walked back to the garage area.

Andretti went on to a convincing victory.

The driver has a part in the mechanical scheme of things. Sometimes, as in the case of A. J. Foyt, he will grab a wrench and dig into the innards of a car's engine right along with the mechanics.

Usually, though, the driver's mechanical task is advisory. The mechanics put things together, but they don't drive the car. Sometimes their work is guesswork. It is up to the driver, then, to tell them how the car is performing.

Only the driver can tell the mechanics that the fuel mixture is too rich, or that the car's steering is bad, or that the rear end does not have the traction it should. Acting on these tips, the mechanics then make what changes they think necessary. It is important that the driver be as specific as possible about what seems to be wrong with the car. A mere "It's not running right" isn't helpful.

Drivers and mechanics often are not the best of friends. Mechanics often complain that drivers abuse their beautiful creations. Drivers often say that their mechanics would have a hard time assembling a coaster wagon. When a team wins, though, everybody acts happy in a hurry, and the mechanics are perhaps happiest of all. For then their beautiful creation has withstood the ultimate test. And they get some of the prize money, too.

6
Balloons, Barbecues, and Broken Hearts

Parnelli Jones sat on the floor, hunched over in a corner of his garage at the Indianapolis Motor Speedway, his face in his hands.

He was suffering, and it showed.

An hour before, Jones had been well on his way to victory in the Indianapolis 500. Driving a turbine-powered car, Jones had a whopping fifty-four-second lead over A.J. Foyt, with only four laps to go.

The year was 1967, and the turbine car was a source of great controversy at the Speedway. Turbine-powered cars had appeared at the Speedway before, but none of them had worked very well. This one was different. It worked extremely well.

It worked so well, in fact, that many drivers, car owners, and mechanics wanted it barred from competition. "The Indianapolis Motor Speedway has always been a proving ground for automobiles — not airplanes," Foyt said.

The car Jones drove wasn't an airplane. But it had much in common with the jets that flew over the Speedway on their way to the Indianapolis Airport. The engine in Jones' car was a turbine, similar to the huge jet engines that powered the big planes.

Because the car made so little noise, compared to the snap, crackle, pop, and roar of the piston engines that powered the other cars in the field, Jones' vehicle was known to most as "The Whooshmobile." He called it Silent Sam.

Silent Sam was the car that was going to carry Jones to his second victory in what the proud promoters of the 500 call the greatest race in the world.

The 500 is a 200-lap race over the two-and-a-half-mile track. Jones, by simply outrunning everyone, had long since made the greatest race in the world the greatest bore of the day as he flashed down the main straightaway after completing the 196th lap.

He never completed the 197th.

Somewhere between the main straight and the backstretch, the quick-change bearing in the car's gearbox quit working, leaving Jones in a car with no gears and no power. Silent Sam had become much too silent.

Jones was able to coast around to the pit area, where he climbed out of the car, turned and looked at it, made a face, then sat on the pit wall and watched Foyt win his race.

By all normal yardsticks, that should have been easy for Foyt. But the Indianapolis Motor Speedway is not normal in any way. Before he was able to win his third Indianapolis victory, Foyt had to thread his way through a four-car crash at the top of the mainstretch on the last lap.

Carl Williams, Bobby Grim, Chuck Hulse, and Larry Dickson hit and spun in all directions, throwing up a huge cloud of dust and smoke.

Foyt, coming around to take the checkered flag of victory, rolled to nearly a complete stop at the side of the track, then finally broke through the smoke and fire-fighting foam. He crossed the finish line at one of

the slowest speeds in history, but to the wild applause of the crowd.

They broke out the champagne for Foyt. Jones sat hunched over in the corner of his garage, his face in his hands.

That's the way it is at the Indianapolis Motor Speedway for the Indianapolis 500. Sometimes. Really, about all that is predictable about the place and the event is that nothing is predictable.

Perhaps that, more than anything else, is the reason for its tremendous popularity.

Besides being a race, though, the 500 is many other things. It is a happening, a gigantic cookout, a one-day vacation. It is whatever three hundred thousand or so spectators choose to make it. And they choose to make it almost anything.

A 500 crowd can nearly always be divided into two separate crowds. There are those who come to see the race, and those who come for something else, whatever it may be. Those who come for the race generally sit in the stands. Those who come for other reasons are generally those who throng the vast infield, which is big enough to have a nine-hole golf course tucked into one corner.

Those who sit in the stands are rather restricted in their activities. They are there to see and be seen. Those who choose the infield have almost limitless possibilities. They have softball games, touch football games, Frisbee games, and card games. They wander about, renewing old acquaintances and making new. They cook on portable grills and nap in sleeping bags. Some of them, it is rumored, even see parts of the race.

The race itself does not start until eleven o'clock in the morning. But the gates are opened at five, giving early arrivals a chance to get in. A good many of those have been up all night, waiting for the gates to open.

Once they get in, they promptly go to sleep, trusting that someone will awaken them for the start of the race — or at least the finish.

In the meantime, Speedway tradition is carefully followed until the race begins. The parade of the race queen and her court around the track is at the same time each year. The Purdue University band marches at the same time each year. And the gaily colored balloons — five hundred of them — are released at the same time each year.

Then, after the band has accompanied a guest celebrity in the singing of "Back Home Again in Indiana," it is magic moment time. The time for the traditional command that starts any American race worth its salt. "Gentlemen, start your engines."

The holiday atmosphere stops for a moment. For an instant, there is silence. An engine roars to life, then others. If all goes well, thirty-three cars — eleven rows of three cars each — are rasping, seemingly eager to get on with it.

Off they go, behind a pace car, for a parade lap and one or two pace laps. The drivers straighten their lines, going at speeds much lower than racing speed, yet much higher than most ordinary people have ever traveled on the ground.

On the backstretch of the final pace lap, the pace car accelerates, pulling away from the snarling pack of race cars, and heads for the safety of the pits.

Necks crane and palms sweat as the field breaks out of the fourth turn toward the starting line. Some fans watch the cars as they swoop into the mainstretch. Others watch to see if the starter will wave the green flag that signifies the beginning of a race.

Some close their eyes and pray.

The start of the Indianpolis 500 is an amazing experience. Thirty-three cars blow past

the stands, their drivers all pushing hard on the throttle. In a way it resembles a herd of cattle stampeding at breakneck speed through a narrow canyon. At the end of the canyon is a turn.

It is tension-choked, and scary enough to raise gooseflesh on the most cynical of observers. It has been described by many as the single most dramatic moment in sports.

The start of nearly any race is high drama. But at Indianapolis, with its hoopla, its month of preparation, its fantastically huge crowd, everything is intensified.

That also includes the danger. With the cars tightly bunched, the drivers all trying to get somewhere in a big hurry, the start is potentially the most dangerous part of the race. An accident then will almost necessarily include more than one car. And accidents at the start are not rare.

Unfortunately, the start of the Indy 500 is often the high point of the race. All too often, it goes from a race to a parade in just a few laps. At speeds near two hundred miles an hour, drivers are not particularly eager to engage in wheel-to-wheel battles. Usually, the idea is to get to the front of the pack and drive as fast as you can for as long as you can, hoping that the car will stand the strain and that nobody will do anything to mess things up.

Race fans understand that. They are willing to put up with the parades because of racing's unpredictable nature. There is no way to tell when a parade is going to be dramatically changed into a real race, with real competition. It is after all, Indianapolis.

Pre-Reading Aids

1

The Drivers

Purpose for Reading

What kind of person drives a race car?

You'll find the answer to this question as you read Chapter 1.

Important Vocabulary

You may find the following words helpful as you read this chapter:

emotions (e mo tions; i mō′ shənz), *n.*
strong feelings

They could not hide their *emotions* as they talked to her after the funeral.

portrayed (por trayed; pôr trād′), *v.*
described, pictured in words

The villain in a story is often *portrayed* as being cruel.

superhuman (su per hu man; sü pər hyü′ mən), *adj.*
divine, beyond normal human power and size

The Greek gods and goddesses were *superhuman.*

resemblance (re sem blance; ri zem′ blən(t)s), *n.*
likeness, similarity in appearance

Her *resemblance* to her sister made it very easy to guess that they were twins.

reflexes (re flex es; rē′ fleks əz), *n.*
the power of reacting with enough speed, acts not controlled by the will

A driver with poor *reflexes* might not move fast enough to avoid an accident.

individualized (in di vid u al ized; in də vij′ u ə līzd), *adj.*
different from each other

Individualized instruction helps all students learn at their own pace.

Pre-Reading Aids

2
The Cruel Sport

Purpose for Reading

What is it that makes auto racing so attractive?

The answer is explored in Chapter 2.

Important Vocabulary

The following words may be of help to you as you read Chapter 2:

temperamental (tem per a men tal; tem pər ə men′ təl), *adj.*
excitable, changeable, high-strung, unpredictable

Actors and actresses are sometimes so *temperamental* that they refuse at the last minute to go onstage.

thoroughbreds (thor ough breds; thėr′ ō bredz), *n.*
things which are well-bred, first-class, or elegant

All of the horses in their stable are *thoroughbreds;* they have been bred and trained especially for racing.

regulate (reg u late; reg′ yə lāt), *v.*
to control, to govern

The floodgates made it possible to *regulate* the amount of water passing through.

distasteful (dis taste ful; dis tāst′ fəl), *adj.*
unpleasant, disagreeable

The job was *distasteful* to him, but he did it because it had to be done.

competence (com pe tence; kom′ pə təns), *n.*
ability and skill

She showed her *competence* as a driver by holding the car steady on the curving road.

immune (im mune; i myün′), *adj.*
protected from

Once you have had measles, you are *immune* from the disease.

thrives (thrives; thrīvs′), *v.*
grows or develops well

The cactus *thrives* in the desert, despite the high temperatures and lack of water.

competition (com pe ti tion; kom pə tish′ ən), *n.*
contest, the effort to obtain something wanted by someone else

The winner of the *competition* received great honor and a very valuable prize.

3
The Indy Car Circuit

Purpose for Reading

Where and when do the Indy cars race?

The answers are in Chapter 3.

Important Vocabulary

The following words may be of help as you read this chapter:

circuit (cir cuit; sėr′ kit), *n.*
a route over which repeated trips are made at certain times

The professional golf *circuit* covers a good part of the country and takes much of the year.

sanctioning (sanc tion ing; sangk′ shən ing), *adj.*
approving, giving permission with authority

That committee is the *sanctioning* committee for all new building in the city; all plans must be approved by them.

easing (eas ing; ēz′ ing), *n.*
gradual moving, taking steps

Easing into the holiday season is difficult; it's always here before we know it.

kink (kink; kingk′), *n.*
a short twist

Joe could not straighten the *kink* in the wire.

prestige (pres tige; pres tēzh′), *n.*
fame, reputation

His *prestige* suffered greatly when it was discovered that he had been lying.

concession (con ces sion; kən sesh′ ən), *n.*
a giving-in, yielding, granting

As a *concession* to them, I agreed not to take part in the activities.

straightforward (straight for ward; strāt fôr′ wərd), *adj.*
honest, without tricks or deceit

Jennifer is a *straightforward* person; you can place your trust in her.

Pre-Reading Aids

4
Who's Got the Money?

Purpose for Reading

Where does the money for Indy car racing come from? Where does it go?

Important Vocabulary

fringe (fringe; frinj′), *adj.*
bordering, on the edges

He was not involved in the theater directly, but was on the *fringe* area where it was important for him to keep track of what was happening.

assured (as sured; ə shürd′), *adj.*
sure, certain

The *assured* marksman had no trouble hitting the bull's-eye.

notorious (no to ri ous; nō tôr′ ē əs), *adj.*
well-known, especially with a bad reputation

The writer had a hard time borrowing money because he was *notorious* for not paying his debts.

endorsement (en dorse ment; en dôrs′ mənt), *n.*
support, approval

Ms. Smith liked that brand of sports equipment so well she was happy to give it her *endorsement.*

obsolete (ob so lete; ob′ sə lēt), *adj.*
out-of-date, old-fashioned, no longer in use

Wooden warships are *obsolete.*

subsidizers (sub si diz ers; sub′ sə dī zərz), *n.*
those who grant aid or money

If it were not for *subsidizers,* many research projects in this country could not be carried on.

accomplished (ac com plished; ə kom′ plesht), *adj.*
skilled, expert

Mr. Jacobs is an *accomplished* cook.

lavished (lav ished; lav′ ishd), *v.*
spent or given very freely

The wealthy father *lavished* gifts upon his three children.

5

My Team, Your Team

Purpose for Reading

Besides cars and drivers, what does it take to make an Indy race?

Important Vocabulary

You may find these words helpful as you read this chapter:

gladiators (glad i a tors; glad′ ē ā tərz), *n.*
persons who fight with great skill; slaves, captives, or paid fighters who fought at public shows in ancient Rome

The *gladiators* were dressed alike, with swords and shields.

sidelines (side lines; sīd′ līnz), *n.*
any businesses carried on apart from that in which a person is chiefly employed

Acting in films is one of his *sidelines;* his main job is playing professional ball.

options (op tions; op′ shənz), *n.*
choices

Students in our school have several *options* in planning what courses they will take.

dominated (dom i nat ed; dom′ ə nāt əd), *v.*
controlled or ruled by strength

Joe Namath was voted the outstanding player because of the way he *dominated* the football game.

maintaining (main tain ing; mān tān′ ing), *v.*
taking care of, keeping up

Maintaining your home in good order will allow you to enjoy it for many years.

advisory (ad vi so ry; ad vī zər ē), *adj.*
concerned with giving an opinion or advice

Her job is *advisory;* she can suggest but cannot direct what they should do.

abuse (a buse ə byüz′), *v.*
to make bad use of, to misuse

If you *abuse* the engine, it is not going to last very long.

Pre-Reading Aids

6
Balloons, Barbecues, and Broken Hearts

Purpose for Reading

What is it like when three hundred thousand or more people get together for the Indianapolis 500?

You'll learn the answer in this chapter.

Important Vocabulary

You may find the following words helpful as you read Chapter 6:

turbine-powered (tur bine pow ered; tėr′ bin pou′ ərd), *adj.*
using the power of a high-speed rotary engine

The *turbine-powered* race cars were much faster than any of the others.

controversy (con tro ver sy; kon′ trə vėr sē), *n.*
disagreement, debate, argument

A *controversy* arose over who should carry the banner in the parade.

predictable (pre dict a ble; pri dik′ tə bəl), *adj.*
expected, able to be guessed

The weather is never completely *predictable;* often it completely changes overnight.

signifies (sig ni fies; sig nə fīz), *v.*
means, makes known, serves as a sign of

To some people, the arrival of the first robin *signifies* that spring is here.

tension (ten sion; ten′ shən), *n.*
stress, mental or nervous strain

Everyone was so worried that you could feel the *tension* in the air.

cynical (cyn i cal; sin′ ə kəl), *adj.*
distrustful, unbelieving

The *cynical* coach didn't believe that Ben could carry the ball without fumbling.

Discussion Questions

Chapter 1

Which of your friends do you think might make the best Indy car driver? Why?

Chapter 2

You've been hired to develop an advertising campaign to promote Indy circuit racing. What approach will you use? What will you emphasize?

Chapter 3

You've been asked to respond to the statement, "If you've been to one Indy circuit race you've been to them all." What will you say?

Chapter 4

Attack or defend the idea that Indy racing is a sport only for the rich.

Chapter 5

If money were not a problem and you had to choose between building your own race car or buying one, what would your choice be? Why?

You've been hired to supervise an Indy racing team. The car owner wants to know what assistants you'll need and why. What will your answer be?

Chapter 6

If you wanted to persuade a friend to go to the Indy 500 with you rather than watch it on TV, what would your argument be?

Related Activities

If Indy-style racing turns you on, you may want to do one or more of the following:

1. Locate the tracks of the Indy circuit on a map of the United States. Label the race sites, including approximate racing dates and the number of miles included in each race.

2. Prepare a tape recording of the sounds of auto racing (Indy racing, if possible). Play this for your class. Explain what the sounds are.

3. Write to each of the Indy racetracks and request a free copy of an official racing program. Make these available to your class.

4. Build a model (original or purchased kit) of an Indy race car. Display this in your class.

5. Write to USAC headquarters: 4910 West 16th Street, Speedway, Indiana 46224. Ask for information about one or more of the following:
   car specifications for Indy-type racing
   the basis for deciding who is qualified to drive in Indy circuit races
   driving rules for Indy-style racing
   the organization and function of USAC
   other matters of interest to you
   Report your findings to your classmates.

6. Create an Indy circuit racing game; use the point scoring system and the calendar of the Indy circuit (described in Chapter 3). Play your game with one or more of your classmates.

7. Visit your school or public library. Find out what resources about car racing (and especially about Indy racing) are available. Post a list and a brief description of these resources in your classroom.

8. Make a mobile or a collage about Indy racing.

9. Watch the local newspapers and national sports magazines carefully for articles about Indy-style racing. Clip some and post them in your class regularly. You may want to report regularly about what is happening.

10. Organize an Indy circuit corner in your room. Display the results of any of these activities—or others—there.

11. Keep a record of the winner of each Indy circuit race this year and of the second, third, and fourth place finishers. Also keep a record of the amounts won and the points earned. Post these regularly for your class.

12. Draw and label diagrams of at least four Indy circuit tracks. Display these. You may want to combine this activity with Activity 3 or Activity 7.

13. Compile a booklet of little-known facts about Indy racing. You may want to combine this activity with Activity 7 or Activity 17.

14. Make a list of one or more of the following and post for the information of your class:
USAC national champions in recent years
Indy circuit earnings of USAC national champions in recent years
Dropouts from last year's Indy 500, including starting positions, finishing positions, laps completed, and reason for dropping out
Fatal accidents on the Indy circuit in recent years

15. Design your own Indy racing car. Prepare side-view, front-view, and top-view drawings or diagrams.

16. Write to each of the Indy circuit tracks. Ask for copies of all free literature about racing there. Make a list of the materials you receive, including a brief description of each item. Post the list and make the materials available for use by your classmates.

17. Obtain a copy of the *Official USAC Auto Racing Yearbook* from the public library. Look through the book. Inform your class what the book contains.

18. Design a poster advertising one of the races on this year's Indy circuit.

19. Make and post a list of official track records for each track of the Indy circuit. Explain differences you discover, either orally or in written form.

20. Obtain biographical information about Indy drivers who interest you. Include information about their performances as drivers during recent years, and a picture of each driver, if possible. Summarize your information and relate it to your class, either orally or in written form.

Reading and Curriculum Editor	Peter Sanders, PhD. Wayne State University
Associate Reading Consultants	John Clark, M.A. Cincinnati Public Schools Cincinnati, Ohio Edward Daughtrey, M.S. Norfolk City Schools Norfolk, Virginia
Story Editor	Patrick Reardon
Associate Editor	Deborah Gardner
Coordinator of Learner Verification	Peter Sanders, PhD.
Related Activities and Vocabulary Sections	Peter Sanders, PhD.
Photography Editor	Eric Bartelt
Graphic Design	Interface Design Group, Inc.
Color Process	American Color Systems
Lithography	A. Hoen & Co.
Binding	Lake Book Bindery

Manufactured in the United States of America to Class A specifications of The Book Manufacturers' Institute

2 3 4 5 6 7 8 9 0   80 79 78 77 76